pearl jam place/date
photography by charles peterson & lance mercer

a vitalogy health club book • Universe

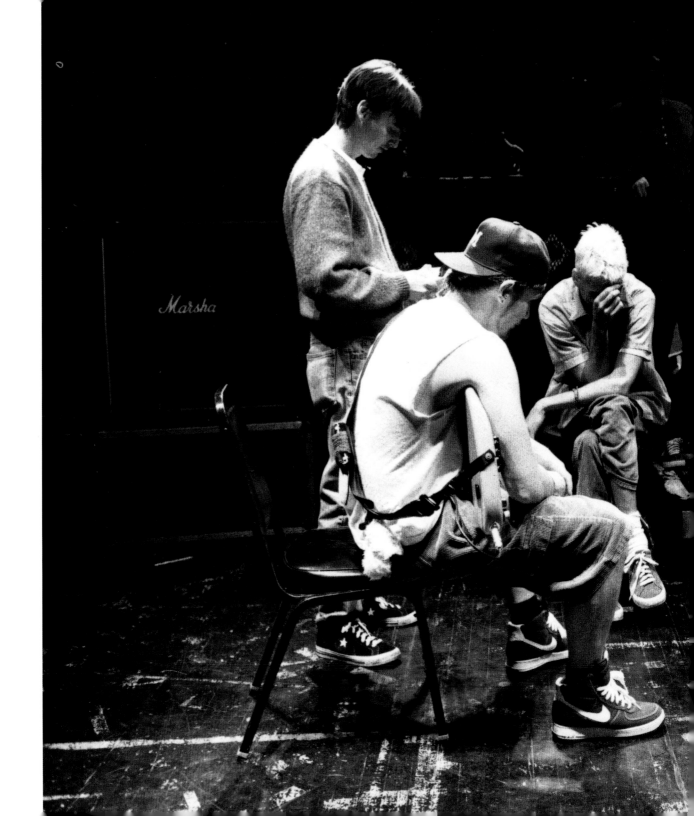

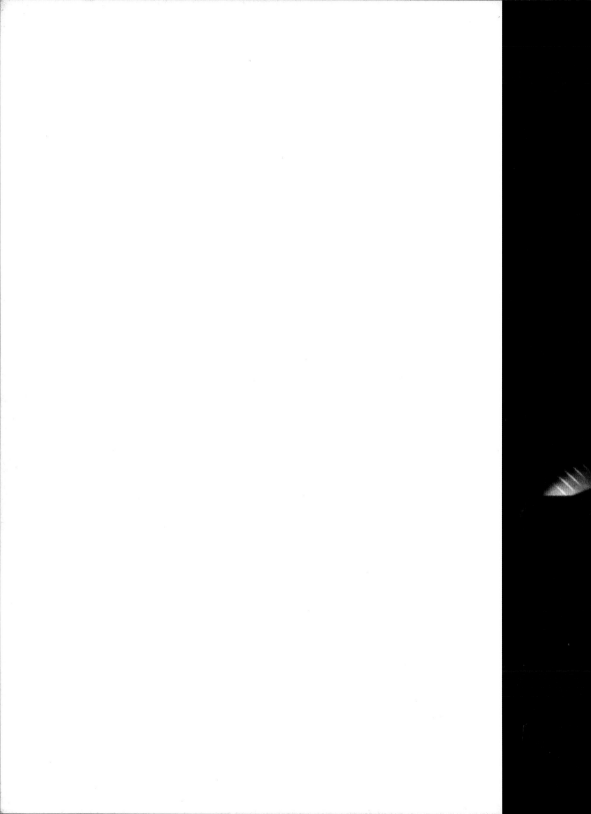

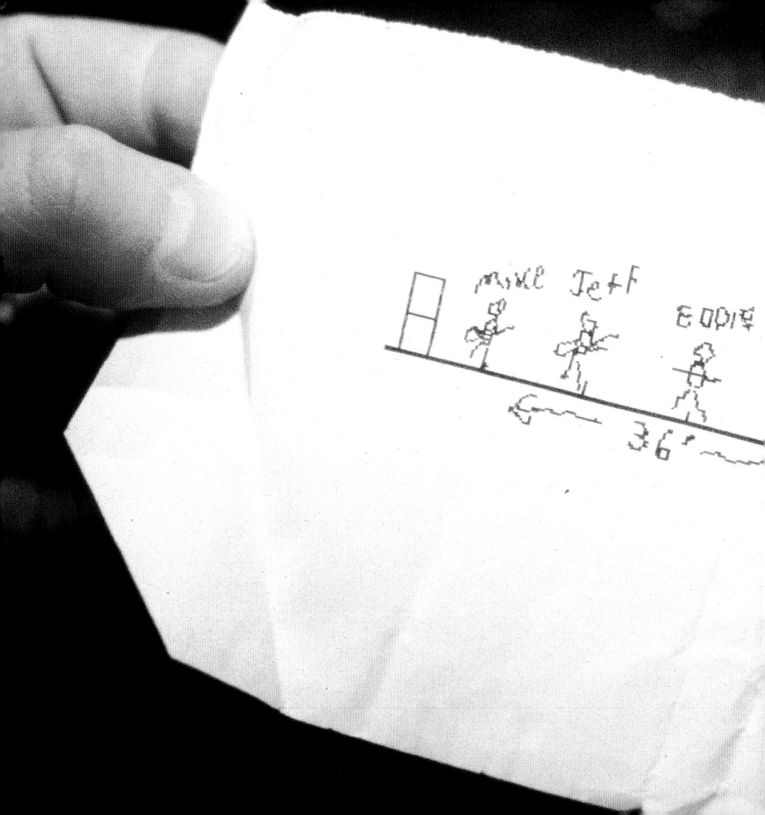

Portland Meadows
Portland, Ore.
1993 / LM

Moore Theater
Seattle
1995 / LM

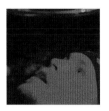

Europe
1993 / LM

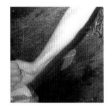

Off Ramp
Seattle
1995 / LM

Shane Castle
1993 / LM

Istanbul
1996 / CP

Charlotte, N.C.
1996 / CP

New York City
1994 / LM

Moore Theater
Seattle
1995 / LM

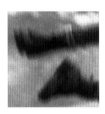

Lollapalooza
Vancouver, BC
1992 / LM

Cascais, Portugal
1996 / CP

Istanbul
1996 / CP

Istanbul
1996 / CP

Istanbul
1996 / CP

Mercer Arena
Seattle
1993 / LM

San Sebastian,
Spain
1996 / CP

Barcelona
1996 / CP

Seattle
1996 / CP

Moore Theater
Seattle
1992 / LM

Last Show at
Chicago Stadium
1994 / LM

Prague
1996 / CP

San Sebastian,
Spain
1996 / CP

Rockcandy
Seattle
1992 / LM

Rockcandy
Seattle
1991 / LM

Spain
1996 / CP

Monkeywrench
Radio #2
Seattle
1998 / CP

Lollapalooza
San Francisco
1992 / LM

Drop in the Park
Seattle
1993 / CP

Drop in the Park
Seattle
1993 / LM

Budapest
1996 / CP

Europe
1992 / LM

Budapest
1996 / CP

Night flight
Budapest to Istanbul
1996 / CP

Off Ramp
Seattle
1995 / LM

London
1993 / LM

Dublin
1993 / LM

Monkeywrench
Radio #1
Seattle
1998 / LM

"Ten"
Seattle
1991 / LM

Off Ramp
Seattle
1995 / LM

Istanbul
1996 / CP

Seattle
1995 / LM

London Bridge
Seattle
1991 / LM

Oakland
1998 / CP

Cascais, Portugal
1996 / CP

Lollapalooza
Irvine, CA
1992 / LM

"Vs."
Olympic Peninsula
1993 / LM

Enroute to San
Sebastian, Spain
1996 / CP

Montreal, CA
1993 / LM

Bewteen Rome
and Dublin
1993 / LM

Cascais, Portugal
1996 / CP

Europe
1993 / LM

Montreal Forum
1993 / LM

Galleria Potatohead
Seattle
1991 / LM

Istanbul
1996 / CP

Eastern Europe
1996 / CP

"Vs."
Olympic Peninsula
1993 / LM

Budapest
1996 / CP

Off Ramp
Seattle
1995 / LM

"Vs."
Olympic Peninsula
1993 / LM

Seattle
1991 / CP

Europe
1996 / CP

Europe
1996 / CP

Mercer Arena
Seattle
1993 / LM

Europe
1996 / CP

Europe
1996 / CP

Moore Theater
Seattle
1995 / LM

Drop in the Park
Seattle
1993 / CP

Drop in the Park
Seattle
1993 / CP

Moore Theater
Seattle
1994 / CP

Prague
1996 / CP

England
1993 / LM

Prague
1996 / CP

Moore Theater
Seattle
1992 / LM

Rockcandy
Seattle
1992 / LM

W/ Lulu, Fastbacks
Caixcais, Portugal
1996 / CP

Barcelona
1996 / CP

Cascais, Portugal
1996 / CP

Cascais, Portugal
1996 / CP

Monkeywrench
Radio #2
Seattle
1998 / CP

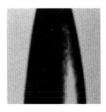

Monkeywrench
Radio #2
Seattle
1998 / CP

Drop in the Park
Seattle
1993 / CP

Cascais, Portugal
1996 / CP

Barcelona
1996 / CP

Boston Garden
1994 / LM

Europe
1993 / LM

Los Angeles
1992 / LM

San Sebastian, Spain
1996 / CP

Mercer Arena
Seattle
1993 / LM

Europe
1993 / LM

Monkeywrench
Radio #2
Seattle
1998 / CP

Seattle
1991 / LM

Boston Garden
1994 / LM

Acknowledgments

Charles Peterson
Special thanks: Ed, Jeff, Stone, Mike and Jack; Kelly and Colleen, Lisa Markowitz, Eric Johnson, Keith Wissmar, Kevin, Dick, Nicole and all the crew. *Extra special thanks:* Hank Trotter, Lance Mercer, Mom, Barkeley and Megan.

Lance Mercer
Pearl Jam, Kelly, Colleen, and everyone at Curtis Management, the P.J. crew (for letting me get in the way). *Special thanks:* Lisa Markowitz, Elyn Sollice and everyone at Epic publicity, E-rock for his support, Keith W. For the light, Hank Trotter for keeping it simple, and Charles Peterson. *Finally and most importantly:* I would like to thank my lovely ladies: Emma, Mackenzie, Evan and my beautiful wife Robyn, whose patience, guidance and loving support helped me persevere.

First published in the United States of America in 1999
by UNIVERSE PUBLISHING
A Division of Rizzoli International Publications, Inc.
300 Park Avenue South
New York, NY 10010

©Pearl Jam, Inc.
Photographs © 1999 Charles Peterson and Lance Mercer.

99 00 01 02 03/ 10 9 8 7 6 5 4 3 2 1

Printed and bound in China through Palace Press International.

Library of Congress Catalog Card Number: 98-61703

ISBN 0-7893-0269-1